WEEKLY **WR** READER®
EARLY LEARNING LIBRARY

My Day at School

# Eating Lunch at School

by Joanne Mattern

Reading consultant: Susan Nations, M.Ed.,
author/literacy coach/
consultant in literacy development

**Please visit our web site at:  www.garethstevens.com**
**For a free color catalog describing Weekly Reader® Early Learning Library's list**
**of high-quality books, call 1-877-445-5824 (USA) or 1-800-387-3178 (Canada).**
**Weekly Reader® Early Learning Library's fax:  (414) 336-0164.**

**Library of Congress Cataloging-in-Publication Data**

Mattern, Joanne, 1963-
    Eating lunch at school / by Joanne Mattern.
       p. cm. — (My day at school)
    Includes bibliographical references and index.
    ISBN-10: 0-8368-6784-X — ISBN-13: 978-0-8368-6784-8 (lib. bdg.)
    ISBN-10: 0-8368-6791-2 — ISBN-13: 978-0-8368-6791-6 (softcover)
    1. School children—Food—Juvenile literature.  2. School children—Juvenile literature.  I. Title.
LB3475.M28    2006
371.7'16—dc22                                      2006005134

This edition first published in 2007 by
**Weekly Reader® Early Learning Library**
A Member of the WRC Media Family of Companies
330 West Olive Street, Suite 100
Milwaukee, WI  53212  USA

Editor: Barbara Kiely Miller
Art direction: Tammy West
Cover design and page layout: Kami Strunsee
Picture research: Diane Laska-Swanke
Photographer: Gregg Andersen

Printed in the United States of America

1 2 3 4 5 6 7 8 9 10 09 08 07 06

## Note to Educators and Parents

Reading is such an exciting adventure for young children! They are beginning to integrate their oral language skills with written language. To encourage children along the path to early literacy, books must be colorful, engaging, and interesting; they should invite the young reader to explore both the print and the pictures.

The *My Day at School* series is designed to help young readers review the routines and rules of a school day, while learning new vocabulary and strengthening their reading comprehension. In simple, easy-to-read language, each book follows a child through part of a typical school day.

Each book is specially designed to support the young reader in the reading process. The familiar topics are appealing to young children and invite them to read — and re-read — again and again. The full-color photographs and enhanced text further support the student during the reading process.

In addition to serving as wonderful picture books in schools, libraries, homes, and other places where children learn to love reading, these books are specifically intended to be read within an instructional guided reading group. This small group setting allows beginning readers to work with a fluent adult model as they make meaning from the text. After children develop fluency with the text and content, the book can be read independently. Children and adults alike will find these books supportive, engaging, and fun!

— Susan Nations, M.Ed., author, literacy coach,
and consultant in literacy development

The school bell rings.

It is time for **lunch**.

I get in line with my class.
We walk to the **cafeteria**,
or lunchroom.  We are quiet
in the halls.

Some children buy lunch.
Today's lunch is pizza.

We can buy milk and juice at school. I like chocolate milk the best.

I brought my lunch from home.  I have a **sandwich**. I have fruit.

Mom packed **pudding**, too!
I love pudding!

15

I sit at a table with my friends.  We eat and talk.

I clean up after I finish my lunch.  I throw away my **trash**.

Lunch is over. We line
up to go outside. Now
we can play!

# Glossary

**buy** — to get something by paying money for it

**cafeteria** — a place where people buy food that is ready to eat

**class** — a group of students who are learning together

**lunch** — a meal eaten in the middle of the day

**pudding** — a sweet, creamy dessert

**sandwich** — two slices of bread with meat or another filling in between

**trash** — things to be thrown away

# For More Information

## Books

*Fruit.*  Let's Read About Food (series).  Cynthia Klingel (Gareth Stevens)

*Milk and Cheese.*  Let's Read About Food (series).  Cynthia Klingel (Gareth Stevens)

*School Lunch.*  True Kelley (Holiday House)

## Web Site

School Lunches
*www.kidshealth.org/kid/grow/school_stuff/school_lunches.html*
Find out what foods are good to bring for lunch at school.

**Publisher's note to educators and parents:**  Our editors have carefully reviewed this Web site to ensure that it is suitable for children.  Many Web sites change frequently, however, and we cannot guarantee that a site's future contents will continue to meet our high standards of quality and educational value.  Be advised that children should be closely supervised whenever they access the Internet.

# Index

## About the Author

**Joanne Mattern** has written more than one hundred and fifty books for children.  Joanne also works in her local library.  She lives in New York State with her husband, three daughters, and assorted pets.  She enjoys animals, music, going to baseball games, reading, and visiting schools to talk about her books.